Published by Scott's Ministry

Some names have been changed in order to maintain the individual's privacy

Scripture is taken from

The HOLY BIBLE, KING JAMES VERSION

Graphic Design and Production
Olmsted Associates, Inc. (Flint, Michigan)

Printed in the United States of America

ISBN-: 978-0-692-29710-0
50699

For more information, please contact:
meleciascott@comcast.net

or visit our **website at: scottsministry.com**

TABLE OF CONTENTS

ACKNOWLEDGMENTS

To God my Heavenly Father, Jesus my Savior, and the Holy Spirit my teacher. Lord I thank you for choosing me as a vessel and entrusting me with this awesome assignment to impart wisdom and knowledge unto your people. Lord I pray for your anointing over this book in Jesus Name! I pray that this book will impact and empower each and every reader. I pray that this book will provide the necessary tools to help each person go forth as soul winners for you! Lord I give you all the glory, honor and praise in Jesus' name.

To my husband Blake Scott, my best friend and partner for life. Blake, I thank God for your unconditional love, your encouraging smile and all your kind words that have helped to strengthen me during this writing assignment. To God be all the glory for your prayers, love and support that helped push me across the finish line, and completing this writing assignment. Thank you Blake for being you! I'm looking forward to our hereafter! I'm looking forward to our greater! I Love You!

To my children. I love you all so very much and thank God for your uniqueness in serving Him in ministry. The Word of God has proclaimed you to be fearfully and wonderfully made, and each of you have been bought with a price. Psalm 127:3 says that children are a gift, and I cherish and honor you all as such. Love, Mom.

To My Mom and Dad, Step-father and Mother-in-Law. I love you all, and I give praise unto God for each of you! I love you, I love you, I love you! And to all my family, I want to say I love you and I thank God for each of you.

To Teri Chambry, God's anointed and humble editor. Sis. Chambry, words cannot fully express my gratitude and appreciation to you, for accepting this editing assignment and treating it as your own. Sis. Chambry you are such a pleasure to labor with in the Kingdom of God. Your spiritual guidance and impartation of wisdom has helped me mature as a writer and as an author, once again. I give my God praise for you sis, and I thank him in advance for rewarding your diligence and faithfulness in this project, working as unto the Lord. Congratulations on your retirement, God bless you sis! Love, Sis. Scott. 1 Corinthians 15:58.

To Barbara Goza. Thank you Sis. Goza for yielding yourself as a vessel in this project to read and check scripture, as well as providing me with feedback. I truly appreciate you and your willingness to be used by God in this assignment. You and your husband have truly been a blessing to me and my entire family over the years and we are so grateful to God for the both of you! Love the Scott family.

To Thelma Day. Sis. Day, I give praise unto God for the wisdom and anointing that flows through you as a servant of God. Thank you for your support, your encouragement, your priceless words of wisdom, as well as for all the wonderful feedback that you provided to me during this project. Blessed woman of God, you have truly made an impact in my life and I will forever be grateful. I give praise unto the Lord for you!

Giving honor and praise to God for my Pastor and his beautiful wife, Margaret. Philippians 1:3 speaks words from my heart as it states, I thank my God upon every remembrance of you. I am grateful for such an awesome man and woman of God to be in my life. Thanking God for you both! Jeremiah 3:15. Love, Sis. Scott.

In Memory Of...

Ernest E. Campbell 1941-2014.
My Step-Father who was a Dad to me starting at age 4 until his death. Thank you Daddy Campbell for loving me as your own. And thank you for being my number one supporter and advocate of *The Meeting*, my first book. You indeed won souls for Christ through that book! Love, your baby girl, Lisa.

Delores Amerson 1963-2014.
My beautiful and sweet cousin, thanking God for you and I will forever cherish our precious moments. I love and miss you Lois.

Chapter One

Why Is The Devil Mad?

"Beep beep beep. We interrupt our regular program schedule to bring you a special report from our news channel."

This is what we often hear as we sit and watch our favorite TV programs: a special news bulletin interrupts and leaves us fidgety and thinking what is going on now? Sitting there on edge watching and listening attentively, we anticipate something negative, just not knowing exactly what. The news anchor or reporter finally appears on the station to introduce himself/herself and then informs us of some type of tragic event. How common is this in our world today? How often do we hear reports of killings, murders, thefts, robberies, kidnappings, rapes, bombings, hi-jackings, weather-related deaths due to hurricanes, earthquakes, tsunamis, terrorist attacks as well as wars over in the Middle East. How numb have we become to the reports of daily killings in our neighborhoods, and in our world? The devil is doing his job...but as Christians...are we?

And so why is the devil mad? The devil (our adversary and enemy) is mad because he knows that his time is running out, or as my pastor says, "It's getting late in the evening."

In Revelation 12:12 it says the devil is come down unto you, having wrath. Satan (the deceiver) is in rage. This verse tells us that the shortness of Satan's opportunity excites his wrath. He works non-stop to destroy the testimony of God's people as well as trying to divert the plans of God. He knows his fate and the plans that God has already decreed for him, and he's mad at all who seeks to follow and do the will of God.

My friends, the devil is not mad at you just because you go to church. No. The devil is mad when you go to the church building with a purpose and made up mind to receive the Gospel message that is preached, and allow it to impact you as well as transform you, then go share it with non-believers. The enemy knows that as you GO you grow! Satan does not want believers to mature in the knowledge of Jesus Christ, the devil does not want you to grow in your relationship with Jesus Christ, instead he wants you to follow the path of religion and the traditions of men which the Bible says makes the Word of God of none effect (Mark 7:13). Victory is always possible for those who follow Christ whether in a life of suffering or be it in death. Our victory is achieved by trusting in the finished work of a crucified Savior and by sticking close to Him through our Christian journey. People of God we are in a spiritual war, a struggle between good and evil, the Kingdom of God and the Kingdom of Satan. And because of this battle…this struggle…this spiritual war that is affecting us all, we should willingly commit and obey the call of the Great Commission that is found in Matthew 28:19-20.

I would like to pose a question: whose side are you on? You are an advocator for which Kingdom? The Great Commission is a command given to the disciples of Jesus Christ. It's an order released upon the followers of Jesus Christ to GO! The Great Commission is Evangelism, also known as Soul Winning, which is witnessing or simply just sharing the Gospel (the life, death, burial and resurrection of Jesus Christ) 1 Corinthians 15:1-4 . Are you willing to GO?

As disciples of Christ, we have been summoned to share the Good News about our Lord and Savior Jesus Christ, thus, providing every person an opportunity to repent (to turn from sin and turn to God), and to believe the Gospel Message through faith. Mark 1:15. Are you willing to GO and share the Good News? And how do we do that? We share it through Evangelism.

Evangelism is the announcement, proclamation, and/or preaching of the Gospel, it is the Good News of and about Jesus Christ. Evangelism is the communication of the Gospel that includes a warning, an explanation, and a call.

The Warning. Warning people about sin and the consequences. Romans 3:23.

The Explanation. An explanation of God's remedy for sin is the Gospel: Jesus' Life, Death, Burial and Resurrection. Through Jesus one can have forgiveness of sins and escape the wrath God, which ultimately leads to eternal separation from Him, meaning hell bound! Romans 10:9-13.

The Call.   A call to receive salvation (deliverance, escape, to be set free from the bondage of sin and eternal death which is God's wrath). Salvation is through Jesus Christ alone. He is our only escape! He is our Way from Satan, our Way from destruction, our Way from darkness leading us to the Way of light, the Way of Truth, the Way of salvation. And Yes, Jesus is the only Way to the Father where we can have the hope of eternal life. John 14:6.

As we prepare our hearts to accept that which God through His Son Jesus has commissioned us to do, we first can begin preparing through learning more about our Savior, Jesus! Example: a new convert sharing the Gospel should know or be familiar with his product, just like a marketer…

- We need to establish a relationship with Jesus Christ: not just knowing about Him but really begin building our relationship through prayer, studying, reading and applying that knowledge learned through everyday life. This building of a relationship will lead us to really know Him.

- We must be optimistic: having FAITH and knowing that Jesus said He is with us. We must stand behind the product, having complete trust and confidence in the Word of God and the Holy Spirit. Speaking truth and standing behind that which we speak. Our body language and heart being in sync with what we speak. If it's a testimony, if it's the Word, say it with confidence and express it with passion.

- We should be enthusiastic about our product: sharing Jesus with joy and fervency, allowing His love to flow through us, and allowing that love to be felt by others. Through Jesus we have been commissioned to GO, and through Jesus we have the anointing to make an impact.

- Finally, we must be real and keep it real: allow the person space, give them time, don't be pushy or over-bearing. Allow them time to open up if they are receptive to the Gospel message. Depending on how the conversation is evolving and if they are engaged, it may be best for us to just to be quiet and listen. It's imperative to follow the Holy Spirit.

Thought to ponder:

The Mission of the Father was to offer hope and salvation to all mankind through His Son Jesus. After Jesus completed his mission on earth he instructed His followers of their mission. (Matthew 28:19-20)

Who should evangelize?

In Matthew 28:18-20 Jesus instructs His disciples regarding their duty after His departure. And Jesus came and spoke to them, saying, "All authority has been given to Me in heaven and on earth. Go therefore and make disciples of all the nations, baptizing them in the name of the Father and of the Son and of the Holy Spirit, teaching them to observe all things that I have commanded you; and lo, I am with you always, even to the end of the age." Jesus has full authority and has commanded us to go. It is His authority that sends us, His authority that guides us, and His authority that empowers us.

Let's take a closer look at this word GO which is a verb and requires action. We are to go and influence unbelievers, sharing the very same message Jesus shared and doing the very same work that He did. So to whom are we to witness? Where should we go? Where are these people that need to hear the

Gospel message? They are everywhere. We are surrounded by people daily. They are all around us wherever we go. In our neighborhoods, at the grocery store, at the movie theater, at the gas station, at the restaurants, in the clubs, at the work place and even in our churches. We must train ourselves to become sensitive to the mission at hand of winning souls for the Christ. Evangelizing should become a part of who we are, allowing ourselves to become natural disciples of Jesus Christ. Winning souls for Christ should be our number one priority in the Kingdom of God. Talking to people on an everyday basis about salvation should become a normal part of our conversation. However, for the majority, approaching one on this subject can often leave us feeling timid, afraid, and embarrassed.

I can recall my first time going door-to-door with our Evangelism Ministry. The leader of the ministry strongly encouraged me to witness to the next person that we approached. Needless to say I was filled with conflicting emotions, thinking WHAT? Fearfully shaking and thinking I don't know what to say. I then took a deep breath and began speaking as the home owner opened the door and said "Hello." Witnessing to my very first convert! God Himself got me through my fears of witnessing on that day and the many days thereafter.

As I reflect and analyze that experience 14 years later, I can attest that fear still visits me periodically before going out to share the Gospel of Jesus Christ, but the difference between then and now is 14 years ago I feared man, but now at this time in my life I fear and reverence God! I know the truth and truth says "fear not them which kill the body, but are not able to kill the soul: but rather fear him which is able to destroy both soul and body in hell" (Matthew 10:28). That is a powerful verse of scripture, and the more I meditate on it and allow God to grow my faith, that scripture is enough to help me overcome my fear factor of NOT saying anything. My silence/disobedience to God can do more harm to me than what any man can do! God is in control. Make disciples of all the nations. The command is to make disciples, not merely converts or supporters of a cause. The idea behind the word disciple is of an adherent, one who accepts the instructions and teachings of Jesus and applies them. A disciple is a pupil, a learner, or a student. This passage of scripture indicates that this command is given to all believers.

To whom should we evangelize?

The scripture says "all nations" (Matthew 28:19-20). Jesus did not ignore, overlook, or reject anyone the opportunity to receive salvation – salvation was made available to all. The Woman of Samaria was a prime example, as found in John 4:1-42.

A Samaritan woman came to the well to get some water and Jesus said to her, "Give me to drink." This happened while His disciples were in town buying food. The woman answered "You are a Jew and I am a Samaritan woman!" (Jews have nothing to do with Samaritans.) Did you catch that? This is a prime example of how we should seek not to be judgmental and avoid any type of discrimination when evangelizing (sharing the Gospel of Jesus Christ). It is for this reason Jesus Himself gives us an example of not exempting anyone the opportunity to receive salvation.

Years ago I can recall the Holy Spirit sending me out one summer day to go witness at a local Kmart in our community. After arriving in the parking lot, I found a spot to park and cut off the ignition to my car, bowing my head in prayer asking God for wisdom and guidance that I may evangelize effectively. While still sitting in my car I gathered some tracts, opened the door to get out, and proceeded to the front of the store near the entrance. I didn't go inside because the Spirit led me to stay outside near the doors. As customers walked past me to enter into the store, one by one, I politely acknowledged them and began a conversation by simply saying, "Hello, how are you today?" Then I asked if they had received Jesus Christ as their personal Lord and Savior, while at the same time handing them a small card with scripture printed on the inside, explaining in depth the plan of salvation and how one may be born again through Jesus Christ.

I had the opportunity to meet and speak with many people. However it was one gentleman who had the most impact on me and taught me an important lesson pertaining to witnessing. As I stood there engaging with various people from many different walks of life it was now time to learn what not to do as a Soul Winner sharing the Gospel of Jesus Christ.

I'm still standing at the front door entrance outside Kmart and here comes a gentleman riding on a motorcycle in rugged biker clothes with a black leather vest, ripped t-shirt, old jeans, a bandanna on his head, biker boots, arms tattooed up and a BIG smile on his face. He parks his motorcycle and begins walking toward me. I thought to myself, "Oh I know he is not a Christian! For sure he's not born again. Let me witness to him!"

"Hello sir, how are you today?" As he walks toward me, the man replies, "I'm doing great!" "My name is Melecia and I am out sharing the Gospel of Jesus Christ today. Have you received Jesus Christ as your Lord and personal Savior?" He replied, Yes ma'am! I most certainly have. I am a Christian and I'm also the proud Pastor of True Saint Community Church of Jesus Christ." I'm saying to myself: What? You're a Pastor? Of course my neck jerked back, my eyes bulged and my mouth dropped. As he saw the expressions on my face he politely smiled and gently replied, "Yes! I'm a Pastor. Smiling, he says, "I get that type of response often, you're not the first one. Let me explain young lady.

You see there are many people out there that I can evangelize and relate to because of my demeanor and how I dress that other Christians wouldn't be able to reach or relate to. The type of ministry that I do allows me to go into the biker clubs, and talk to the bikers about Jesus Christ and salvation. I don't wait for them to walk into the Church building, because some of them never will." "Ok, yes, yes, Amen!" I said, nodding my head in agreement and looking on in amazement. Then he reminds me of the scripture in 1 Corinthians 9:19-23 that says, "For though I be free from all men, yet have I made myself servant unto all, that I might gain the more. And unto the Jews I became as a Jew, that I might gain the Jews; to them that are under the law, as under the law, that I might gain them that are under the law; To them that are without law, as without law, (being not without law to God, but under the law to Christ,) that I might gain them that are without law. To the weak became I as weak, that I might gain the weak: I am made all things to all men that I might by all means save some. And this I do for the Gospel's sake, that I might be partaker thereof with you." "Yes, Amen!" I said. "So young lady," he said, "you keep on sharing the Gospel of

Jesus Christ, you're doing a good job! Be encouraged!" I said, "Thank you, sir! Thank you for taking the time to talk with me, as well as imparting wisdom. Have a blessed day! Bye!" He responded simply, "Bye young lady!"

Standing there in amazement, my heart melted as the Holy Spirit ministered to me on this crucial evangelistic lesson, a lesson that would be life changing for me and to others as well.

Now you ask, what was the lesson? The lesson was to never call judgment on anyone from looking at their outward appearance to determine the status of their salvation or their love for Jesus Christ. Scripture reminds us that man looks upon the outward appearance but God looks at the heart (1 Samuel 16:7).

Thought to ponder:

Be not forgetful to entertain strangers: for thereby some have entertained angels unawares. (Hebrews 13:2)

Chapter Two

We All Need Encouragement

We are human and we all need encouragement. Jesus teaches us yet once again as we look at the Samaritan woman and see the Master Soul Winner and encourager at work. In this chapter we observe the various methods Jesus used with the Samaritan woman at the well. John 4:6-7 says as the Lord Jesus was sitting by the well, a woman came out from the village to draw water. Jesus knew what she needed and He was determined to meet her at the very place that represented what she was missing – living water/spiritual life – she needed salvation.

The Samaritan woman went to draw water daily to quench her physical thirst not knowing the drought in her soul was longing for so much more. She was longing for things that could only satisfy her temporarily. She had no idea that Jesus was that spiritual fountain from which she could draw from continuously to satisfy her spiritual longings and so much more! This woman not only needed encouraging but she needed salvation.

As the Samaritan woman approached Jesus, by no means was he intimidating or derogative to her. It is for this very reason she felt comfortable in

His presence to listen. When the Prince of Peace is at work, troubled minds and hearts can experience rest even in the midst of turmoil. Look at Jesus…not only is He making a spiritual deposit but He is making a withdrawal, Jesus is allowing the Samaritan woman time to confess her sin, so that He can make a spiritual deposit.

Let's pause right here and reflect knowing that we can identify with this woman for we all long for things that temporally satisfies us. One of my daily temporary longings in the past was compulsive shopping. As a babe in Christ, newly married and a young mother of two I was walking with Christ, only walking with Him from a distance during this time in my life. I remember oh so well how after our wedding, my husband and I begin to focus solely on getting established in our marriage, our home, our careers and our new family – totally immersing ourselves in these daily affairs and neglecting our spiritual life. My husband's church attendance, as well as mine, dropped drastically, later leading to us not going to church at all. My life now feeling empty and void I soon began immersing myself with shopping. Yes! Uncontrollably shopping, spending money, using credit cards, secretly using my husband's credit card without permission, buying any and everything in eye sight. A time in my life that was supposed to be joyful: a new marriage, a new home, babies, etc., turned my spirit into sadness and thirst. Soon this spiritual thirst affected me emotionally, mentally, and socially. I soon began a quest to quench and satisfy my thirst through things and in people but only finding temporary satisfaction. You see the more I bought the more I wanted, the more I wanted and couldn't have, the angrier I became. This went on for years and soon began to affect my marriage and everyone around me.

Feeling like an emotional wreck and clueless to the root of my problem or the solution to it, I became grumpy and insensitive which caused me even more frustration. People of God, it was only after God sought me out and brought me back to Him that my life changed for the better. You see it was one day while in our living room my husband and I were talking and God brought it to our attention that it had been five years since we had last went to church, read a Bible or anything, and that it was time for us to get back into fellowship with Him and the saints so that our spiritual thirst and spiritual longings could be quenched through Him. The Bible tells us that no earthly possession could ever satisfy us completely without Jesus. Ecclesiastes reminds us in 2:11 "and, behold, all was vanity and vexation of spirit, and there was no profit under the sun." Without God there is no lasting satisfaction!

Now back to the woman at the well. Jesus is at the well and asked the woman for a drink. Jesus says, "Give me to drink." She then recognized Jesus as a Jew and is amazed that He would even speak to her.

Do we know how many people feel that way that live in our communities? People feel ostracized by church people. Many shun away from the church building as well as accepting a personal relationship with Jesus Christ simply because of a misconception of Christians. We as Christians are human and we err in our ways. Oftentimes we don't represent Christ in the manner in which we should on a day-to-day basis. However, God forgives us, and as disciples of Jesus Christ, the Holy Spirit continuously teaches us when we yield ourselves to Him. This is an important step: we must continue being a student under Jesus the Master Teacher, for this is the only way we can expand our knowledge and grow that we will become better equipped for the work of the church.

Let us sit down at our desk as disciples and look unto our Master Teacher Jesus. Our teacher schools us on approaching the unsaved. Here we see "LOVE" in action. Let's take a look.

Lesson One

In John 4:4 it says that Jesus intentionally took this route to meet the woman at a place in which she was very much familiar. Believers need to be willing to go where the unsaved are. This may require us to go in areas or places that are not familiar to us but a place that is familiar to the unsaved. A place of comfort for them could very well be a place that is not comfortable for us. However, Jesus went to her, He did not wait for her to walk up into the temple. Even as we begin witnessing and speaking the Gospel truth, we need to be cautious of our word choice. In our conversation it is vital to speak words that the unsaved can relate to and understand.

I can recall being on the battlefield, embarking onto the streets of my community with other Soul Winners targeting an area in our community that was drug infested and highly solicited by prostitutes. As we approached the area in our vehicles, my adrenaline was pumping and my heart was pounding. I was excited and yet nervous not knowing what to expect. After noticing a few people on the street, our team carefully approached them after exiting our cars. To my right I noticed a woman who appeared to be in distress. I approached her slowly and carefully, but at the same time keeping my distance, while waving my hand and introducing myself with a friendly voice. "Hi, how are you today? I asked,

"Sweetie are you ok?" She looked at us and said nothing. The woman was not receptive to us in the beginning, for it was obvious that she was craving for whatever substance that she was on and she had little to no conversation for us. As I briefly spoke with her, gently saying, "Jesus loves you," she began pouring out her emotions of anger on me as to why her life was in shambles. I tried to console her the best I could but it only made matters worse. The more I talked the angrier she became. I felt she just needed someone to listen, so I listened to the point where she began answering her own questions, becoming even angrier at herself and me. She later stormed off and yelled, "I don't want your help, can't nobody help me!"

Even though this young lady was not receptive to us, there were many who were. We took the love of Jesus Christ to them. That same night as I was ministering to that young lady, one of the other ladies in our Soul Winning group was ministering to a young lady who was a prostitute. We later learned that she surrendered herself to God and accepted Jesus Christ as her Lord and Savior. Over time this lady was delivered by the power of God and began serving Him in ministry! What a Mighty God we serve!

Lesson Two

We now see that Jesus, the Master Teacher, purposely chose this day to speak with her alone, the disciples were not there, they had journeyed to a nearby village to buy food, which allowed Jesus quality one-on-one time with the Samaritan woman.

People of God, in no way should we seek to embarrass the person that we're speaking with. Jesus made arrangements to speak with this woman alone. He did not expose her sins before others or condemn her. Jesus displayed love and compassion to this sinner as well as privacy. Jesus' mission was salvation and this private moment would later lead to a public confession that Jesus is Lord, for after this encounter, did not this woman run into town shouting to all "Come see a Man who told me all I ever did!"

Jesus' mission was to give her a taste and later fill her with living water, i.e., *Salvation/Eternal Life*. At that moment a taste was all that was needed. A taste was enough to quench her thirst and become curious and thirsty for more. Saints give them a taste, the world needs to taste Christ through us. Jesus said that we are the "salt of the earth." They not only need to see, but they need to taste the Gospel message through us. Allow sinners to taste what forgiveness is like through you...allow sinners to taste love through you…allow sinners to taste humility through you. You don't have to give them a big bite, just give them a taste.

Lesson Three

Jesus allowed the woman to make spiritual withdrawal from Him. The sinner comes to us empty, they come to us thirsty and searching to fill that void in their life. As Soul Winners, it is important for us to know that we cannot quench their thirst or fill their void. However, we can point them to the One who can. We can be a spiritual compass or GPS for them, navigating them to the fountain who is Jesus…a well that springs forth living water and this fountain will never run dry.

Lesson Four

The Samaritan woman was also searching for love, the very thing that she was seeking in her many relationships and was never fully satisfied. Jesus was that missing piece – that missing link in her life, for He has the power to appease anything that is missing or lacking in our lives.

Jesus continues to speak to her in love, eliminating the communication barrier, the very thing that she had struggled with for so long with others. Is it possible that this woman longed to communicate her various issues with others, maybe even with those to whom she had a relationship, but was unsuccessful due to reputation? Reputation or not, Jesus took the time to demonstrate true love in action: a love that listened, a love that took time to give counsel and speak healing, and lastly, a love that was persistent. He patiently engaged the Samaritan woman drawing her closer to Him with the goal of wooing her soul, knowing that she already had a desire to connect to the well springs of life. Through this conversation, it brought her to a place of conviction which later led her to a deeper place of curiosity pertaining to spiritual matters. And this provided Him the opportunity to speak truth and provide light to her darkened understanding. Oh, the power of love.

In Proverbs 20:5 it says that "Counsel in the heart of man *is like* deep water; but a man of understanding will draw it out." Jesus helped this woman see her need for salvation. He helped her to understand her life of sin and a need for a Savior. He didn't demean her or speak to her in a condemning way but just simply pointed her to *The Way of Salvation*...gave her *The Truth* about her situation...and offered her eternal *Life, Living Water*. Understanding God and His ways with us can help make us more sensitive while ministering to others. Jesus is willing to meet us where we are and to bring us out of a spiritual drought into overflowing springs that has the capacity to flood our souls (give us joy) as we experience *The* eternal fountain. Try Jesus for

He is truly that endless and everlasting fountain that never runs dry.

Remember this!

- Jesus did not place Himself above her (the sinner)
- Jesus engaged her in the conversation
- Jesus spoke in love
- Jesus listened

Thought to ponder:

For all have sinned, and come short of the glory of God; (Romans 3:23)

Chapter Three

Exposing The Enemy

Let us reveal who the real enemy is as followers of Jesus Christ. What our enemy, Satan, does not want us to know about him is that:

- ***He is a deceiver.*** He will do anything in his power to blind the mind of the unbeliever so that they do not believe the Gospel of our Lord Jesus Christ. This includes changing the Gospel, or watering it down so that people who think they are hearing the truth are really being deceived and blinded to the pure Gospel message. Only the power of God can remove the blinders put on by Satan, allowing one to hear, receive and believe God's perfect pure Word.

- ***He is the master of confusion.*** And his goal is to pervert the Word of God. Pervert means to distort or change something from its original or intended use. Satan aims at distorting what has been given by God to man for his blessing and benefit. Many times Satan distorts the truth of God's Word so that man has a misunderstanding of some important

29

attributes of God or His glorious Gospel. This is one of Satan's top goals. He hopes he can lead believers astray rather than growing in the grace and knowledge of our Lord and Savior Jesus Christ.

- ***He is a liar.*** The Bible tells us that Satan is the father of lies and a liar by character (John 8:44). Therefore, he is never trustworthy or believable. Satan has lied since the beginning of time when he convinced Eve to eat of the tree in the midst of the garden, telling her that she surely would not die. This was a lie…from the mouth of Satan to Eve.

  Only Jesus has the power to help us know and discern Biblical truth from Satan's lies. When we are faced with confusion, He is able to give us understanding and when we are blinded or in doubt, He is well able to help us see things clearer.

Knowing our enemy and *knowing about* our enemy is vital to living a victorious and an abundant life as a Christian. Jesus said in John 10:10, "The thief cometh not, but for to steal, and to kill, and to destroy: I am come that they might have life, and that they might have it more abundantly." In this scripture John is speaking to believers, and he is exposing three of Satan's characteristics:

- To steal – Satan attempts to secretly steal away our hearts from our Lord.
- To kill – by false doctrines and poisoning the minds of believers.
- To destroy – abolish (end, finish, extinguish, terminate) any hope of life believers would have in our Lord. And for unbelievers his goal is *permanent* (absolute) destruction, i.e., to cancel out (remove); to die, with the implication of ruin and *destruction*; because to be *lost* (*utterly* perish) is to spend eternity in hell. Yes my friends, Satan wants company in hell with him!

Let's take a closer look. The scriptures and the characteristics listed below will help us further in our effort to learn more about Satan's character.

Understanding the nature and tactics of Satan, knowing and receiving what the scripture says about him is important. Starting with 1 John 5:19 that says, "...the whole world lieth in wickedness."

2 Corinthians 11:14-15 "...for Satan transforms himself is transformed into an angel of light. Therefore it is no great thing if his ministers also be transformed as the ministers of righteousness; whose end shall be according to their works."

1 John 4:1 "Beloved, believe not every spirit, but try the spirits, whether they are of God; because

many false prophets are gone out into the world..."

Ephesians 6:10-18 "...be strong in the Lord and in the power of His might. Put on the whole armor of God, that you may be able to stand against the wiles of the devil. For we wrestle not against flesh and blood, but against principalities, against powers, against the rulers of the darkness of this world, against spiritual wickedness in high places. Wherefore take unto you the whole armor of God, that you may be able to withstand in the evil day..."

"Stand therefore, having your loins girt about with truth, and having on the breastplate of righteousness. And your feet shod with the preparation of the Gospel of peace; Above all, taking the shield of faith wherewith ye shall be able to quench all the fiery darts of the wicked. And take the helmet of salvation, and the sword of the Spirit, which is the word of God: Praying always with all prayer and supplication in the Spirit, and watching thereunto with all perseverance and supplication for all the saints."

1 Peter 5:8 "Be sober, be vigilant; because your adversary, the devil, as a roaring lion, walketh about, seeking whom he may devour."

Ephesians 4:26-27 "Be ye angry, and sin not: let not the sun go down upon your wrath: Neither give place to the devil."

Revelation 20:10 "And the devil that deceived them was cast into the lake of fire and brimstone, where the beast and the false prophet *are*, and shall be tormented day and night forever and ever."

1. Plans to steal, kill and destroy. (John 10:10)

2. Rules the masses *outside* God's protection. (Eph. 2:1-3)

3. Keeps seeking an "opportune time" to tempt us. (Luke 4:13)

4. Tries to hide the actual truth about our God. (2 Cor. 4:3-4)

5. Offers counterfeit promises he can't fulfill. (Gen. 3:4-5)

6. Twists Scriptures to fit his purposes. (Gen. 3:1-5)

7. Will be cast into the lake of fire and brimstone. (Revelation 20:10)

A little later in this chapter we will complete an assignment to expose some of the traps, lies and methods that Satan uses to prevent us from moving forward, aspiring to fulfill the Great Commission as well as living that abundant life that Jesus offers.

As we discuss our fears we need to understand that there are healthy fears as well as unhealthy fears. The fears that I am speaking about are those unhealthy fears that prevent us from doing the work of the church, evangelizing and winning souls for Christ.

It is that unhealthy fear that controls us and consumes us. It robs us of the joy and abundance of life that God has intended for us. Fear is a double-edged sword; it can save us, and it can destroy us. How can we preserve the place of healthy fear in our lives, and protect ourselves from the death-dealing effects of unhealthy fear? The first thing we need to do is face our fears. What is plaguing you to the point that it is preventing you from moving forward to what Jesus has called you to do and from fulfilling the Great Commission or any mission for that reason? Fear: get thee behind me in Jesus' name!

Over the past few years, my husband and I have been blessed with many opportunities to host workshops for our churches' Evangelism Ministry. In each of those workshops we ask our classroom participants to name some of the fears that have plagued them or prevented them from going out to witness, sharing the Gospel of Jesus Christ. The response to this question is almost always the same. Below I have listed a few of those responses/fears. They are:

- Fear of not knowing enough about the Bible, being asked something and not knowing the answer
- Fear of rejection; not being received
- Fear of approaching people
- Fear of what others will think
- Fear of being teased or talked about
- Fear of being ostracized
- Fear of not knowing what to say
- Fear of making a mistake
- Fear of being on the streets
- Fear of confrontation

The list can go on and on.

Were any of your fears listed above? Do you have other fears you would like to add to the list above? Go ahead, list as many as you can think of. This lesson was designed to help every person examine the fear factors in their life. I want you to dig deep within your basket of fears so they can be washed away with the Word and hang them out to dry putting them all in perspective. Example, if your fear is being afraid that people will reject or despise you, let's first begin by replacing the YOU with Jesus!

The scripture says in Luke 10:16, "He that heareth you heareth me; and he that despiseth you despiseth me; and he that despiseth me despiseth him that sent me." Brothers and sisters we are

Representatives for Jesus, every time we witness to someone, we are acting on His behalf. Yes we are human and yes we have feelings, however, we need to have the mindset that those who reject us, really are rejecting Christ, so do not take it personal.

Daily we go to the work place and represent our company to the best of our ability. Some of us are obligated to completing classes to train for the job, attend workshops, become certified, take classes, or just be persistent and show forth commitment to represent our company in the best possible way we can. My point is we need to have that same zeal and commitment while sharing His Gospel as representatives for Jesus Christ. Understanding that obeying the call of the Great Commission is the most important duty we have as disciples of Jesus Christ and our reward awaits those of us who choose to obey!

As we continue with this subject, today is the day we need to make a choice to face our unhealthy fears and begin to speak faith to these dead works. Today is the day for us to decide to take a stand and go toe-to-toe with our fears, declaring the Word of God over them so that we can walk victoriously as a disciple of Jesus Christ. Are you ready?

On the next page is an exercise I would like you to try…and I hope it will prove to be helpful.

LIST YOUR FEARS OF WITNESSING	LIST WHAT GOD'S WORD SAYS ABOUT THAT FEAR

<u>Notes</u>

Chapter Four

Empowering The Believer

Now that you have listed your fears, you noticed that we are in a new chapter. We left our fears in the last chapter. We have chosen to move on. We accept what the Word of God says, understanding that we have continuously meditated upon those scriptures and reminded ourselves of what the Word of God says in faith vs. how we feel in our flesh.

Your flesh (your mind) is saying nothing has changed. You are still a failure. You are still afraid. But you will have to speak the Word of God to that spirit of fear daily, to keep him in check! 2 Timothy 1:7 says, "For God hath not given us the spirit of fear." Don't continue to suffer in silence and be tormented by Satan. Yes, he has a team. But you have a team and your team is, by far, the Greater! The Greatest team in eternity: the Almighty God, Jesus the Christ, and the Power of the Holy Ghost are all on your team. And…you have a host of angels to hearken at your command. Don't allow the enemy victory in your life by preventing you from being productive in the Kingdom of God. Now if you want you can go back and stay in chapter three, that's where Satan wants you, STUCK. Or you can accept and receive what the scriptures say about your fear and/or fears, and by faith daily fight and declare I am moving on in Jesus Name!

Okay, are you *ready* to move on? Remember this is a daily decision, not a onetime fix. Now that we have *disclosed* our fears, it's time to *depart*. Are you ready to enter into the next phase of your life?

Are you sick and tired of being stuck? Envision yourself doing the very thing that you're afraid to do. Close your eyes and envision that victory, whatever it is. Wow! Didn't that feel good to actually see yourself doing the very thing that Satan has continuously tried to stop you from doing! The Bible says that we are more than conquerors in Romans 8:37 please read it for yourself. Now to envision is only the first step, and to actually do it, is another step. And remember, it's a start because we all have first times for everything. I can recall my first time riding a bike, how I fell off countless times. I can recall my first kiss, oh how awkward. I can recall my first time speaking publicly, oh my goodness I thought I was going to throw-up or pass out or both. However, the feeling, the fear didn't stop me. God helped me to press through the fears later feeling fearless until it was time to do it again. This is your time to begin your beginning.

This chapter is where we will be empowered, through *disengaging* – to withdraw or mentally separate ourselves from these fears through faith in what God has already said about the situation. And then renewing our minds as the Word of God says in Romans 12:2 and replacing those negative thoughts with the Word of God as found in Ephesians 5:17 "Therefore do not be foolish, but understand what the Lord's will is."

As Believers we have been given authority through Jesus Christ in Matthew 28:18: "Jesus came and spake unto them, saying, all power is given unto me in heaven and in earth." When we made Jesus Christ Lord of our life, Colossians 1:13 says you were delivered from the power of darkness. The Word *power* is literally translated "authority." You have been delivered from the power, or authority, of darkness and placed into God's kingdom.

By going to the cross, dying a horrible death, suffering the penalty for sin and defeating Satan, Jesus came to earth and recaptured the authority Satan had stolen through disobedience in the Garden. Jesus was called the last Adam (I Corinthians 15:45). After securing that power and authority, He freely gave it over into the hands of those who would believe on Him.

Jesus has declared for us to "Go ye into all the world, and teach all nations." Every born-again believer has the authority and responsibility to share the Gospel of Jesus Christ in this earth.

Ephesians 4:27 says, "Neither give place to

the devil." In Ephesians 6, the Apostle Paul describes the armor that we as believers are to wear in combat against Satan and He explains each piece of that armor. It is the armor of God. However God will not put the armor on for you. It is your responsibility and duty as a believer to put on the armor of God and stand against the devil, refusing to be moved. God has already provided everything that we need for this spiritual fight. The armor and the weapons are tools provided and given to us by God and should not be left hidden in our lives, but instead should become active and alive through our faith, that we may defeat the enemy, Satan. Saints, we have the authority to take the Word of God, in the Name of Jesus by the power of the Holy Spirit and take command over Satan and his demons. Yes, we have been given authority in the name of Jesus! Take your position in Christ and speak boldly to the enemy. James 4:7 gives us instructions on how to do this. James says submit yourselves therefore to God. Resist the devil, and he will flee from you. That word submit means to rank under, to be under obedience, to obey, to put under, to be in subjection under, to submit unto.

James reminds us that we are always engaged in a conflict between the devil's control and God's. We have to choose to submit and position our lives under God's direction. It is an immediate demand, it is a call for voluntary submission to God and His will. This is a very hard thing for the proud to do for it is a complete humbling. It is hard for all of us to do because we all struggle with pride: the devils' focal point. However, the Word of God reminds us in Luke 18:27 that "The things which are impossible with man are possible with God."

Helpful Words to Know

- Sin – Missing the mark (missing the mark of God's standard of righteousness); disobedience.

- Convert – To change the opinion or beliefs of someone.

- Salvation – God's rescue which delivers believers out of eternal destruction and into His safety. God rescuing believers from the penalty and power of sin. Deliverance from sin or the consequences of sin through Jesus Christ's death on the cross, saved from the wrath of God and the 2nd death.

- Reconciliation – To change from enmity or disharmony to friendship and harmony or in short, reconciliation is the whole work of God in Christ by which man is brought from the place of enmity to peace with God and can be restored to fellowship with a Holy God through His Son Jesus Christ.

- Sanctification (progressive) – This is a *lifelong process* and work of the Holy Spirit where the believer is brought closer to the likeness of Christ through **obedience** to the Word of God and the empowering of the Holy Spirit. It is through sanctification that the believer is able to live a life of increasing holiness in conformity to the Will of God becoming more like our Lord Jesus Christ.

- Justification – Justification removes the guilt and penalty of sin when the sinner trusts in Christ as his or her Savior, God declares him or her to be righteous, and that declaration will never be repealed nor will it ever need to be repeated. This is instant and permanent. Justification exempts us from the Great White Throne judgment (this is where the unsaved go for judgment after death), whereas progressive sanctification prepares us for the Bema, the Judgment Seat of Christ, and the blessings of rewards.

- Redemption – Buying back, delivering, restoring; purchasing us from the debt of sin and bringing us into our new status of being in Christ.

- Propitiation – Propitiation is the doctrine or truth that the person and death of Jesus Christ appeased (turned away), God's wrath, satisfied

His holiness, and met God's righteous demands that the sinner can be reconciled into God's holy presence. Jesus was the only one who could meet the just demands of our Holy God, so that we become acceptable to God through Jesus.

- Glorification – The future and final work of God upon Christians where He transforms our mortal physical bodies to the eternal glorified bodies in which we will dwell forever. 1 Cor. 15:42-44.

We have all sinned and deserve God's judgment. God, the Father, sent His only Son, Jesus, to satisfy that judgment for those who believe in Him. Jesus lived a sinless life, He loves us so much that He willingly died for *our* sins, taking the punishment that we deserve, was buried, and rose from the dead according to the Bible. If you truly believe and trust this in your heart, receiving Jesus alone as your Savior, declaring, "Jesus is Lord," you will be saved from judgment and spend eternity with God in heaven.

Chapter Five

Engaging Others

So how can we engage others in this movement of Soul Winning? The answer is not that simple. Jesus has given us the command but it's up to us individually to obey it or rebel against it, each person has to decide and make a choice to engage in this spiritual fight.

Brothers and sisters we can clearly see that we are in a battle – a battle of good and evil. However, many people feel there is no need to get involved and they ask what impact can I make? Some may feel they don't have enough knowledge about the Bible, and as for witnessing, isn't that the preacher's responsibility? – that's not my calling. And to others it appears we are already outnumbered as we view many hopeless and impossible situations (from a natural perspective),wondering if one person can really make a difference. How about the response of just let someone else do it! I'm busy and I don't have time.

Dear ones, these negative responses and negative thoughts are in reality, excuses searching for an escape of our Christian responsibility to obey the Great Commission commanded to us by Jesus

Christ. These faithless thoughts grip us, later plaguing our mind and oppressing our will, making it almost impossible to choose to get engaged. This negativity influences us strongly to stay disengaged which leads to passivity and ultimately preventing us from performing our purpose of winning souls for Christ in any given situation presented to us.

After we fall for the trap of feeling we are not needed and maybe feeling too nervous or neglected and unsure due to our own life issues, we take the escape route. We then begin to gravitate to other matters, immersing ourselves with things that have no lasting value. However committing ourselves to witnessing and sharing the Gospel of Jesus Christ has eternal value, as well as being a life or death, heaven or hell situation. The truth is that many have died not hearing the Gospel message. Many have come upon near death experiences, having visions to awaken them to God's pure Gospel Truth. Luke 16:24 is a reminder to us all about the power of choice, and the urgency of knowing the pure Gospel message of Jesus Christ, and the consequences of rejecting it. Here is a quote from that passage of scripture; "And he cried and said, Father Abraham, have mercy on me, and send Lazarus, that he may dip the tip of his finger in water, and cool my tongue; for I am tormented in this flame."

Yes dear ones, it is crucial that we share this Gospel message with everyone: our family, our friends, our loved ones, neighbors and with strangers when led to do so. Below I would like to share some real life testimonies and I'm sure you have a few of your own.

Testimony 1. The summer of 2014 a young girl recently had her faith shaken as she went to a party without her parents' permission only to find herself in the middle of cross-fire. She began begging and pleading for God to save her life. As the bullets crossed her flying through the air while frantically trying to get into her friend's car, the front windshield was quickly pierced by bullets shattering it into a million pieces and leaving her stuck while lying on the ground crying, shaking and screaming for her life. The gunmen began to re-load their ammunition and it was at that moment she and her two friends seized the opportunity to crawl into the car, starting the ignition and then speeding off as bullets continued to fly in the air traumatizing them all! Our children need us to get involved!

Testimony 2. My neighbor, who is a faithful, God-fearing woman, was at home alone one evening watching television when someone began banging on her front door. A young man was screaming for help, begging her to call 911 because he had been shot. Immediately Ms. Ruth called 911 shaking and afraid as she continued hearing gun fire outside her door. The young man laid there until the ambulance arrived and attended to his medical needs. He was taken to the hospital immediately, miraculously surviving his injuries. Our children need us to get involved!

Testimony 3. *On a beautiful sunny day in mid-afternoon my son and his friend had just finished choir practice and the two of them had decided to walk home. Enjoying the warm sun, walking, laughing and making plans for the next day not really paying attention to their surroundings, a gunman suddenly appeared before the two of them attempting a robbery. The robber put a gun to my son's head and demanded money and any valuables he had. Ricky didn't have any money just a cell phone, so the robber took that and then fled on foot leaving the two of them shaken and afraid. Soon Ricky arrived home and shared his testimony with us, giving Praise to God for protecting him and his friend. We all began thanking God for sparing his life! Christian Believers, we need to get involved!*

Daily we hear about different tragic stories – many affecting our own families, and loved ones. Saints, it's time to get involved! It's time to take this Gospel message to the streets, sharing the message daily as we do our normal everyday tasks as it is just as equally important for us to live it. Jesus has already warned us in the scripture that there is a time coming when the father shall be divided against the son, and the son against the father; the mother against the daughter, and the daughter against the mother; the mother-in-law against her daughter-in-law, and the daughter-in-law against her mother-in-law (Luke 12:53). Christian Believers, it's time to get involved!

I have had the opportunity to mentor many troubled youth, gaining their confidence and trust through various mentorship programs. Many youth have confided in me about various experiences they have encountered. The one thing that impacted me the most was when they expressed a void of love and acceptance that they felt was lacking in the home as well as an absence of spiritual guidance or any guidance for that matter. These young men and women longed for love and attention. However, due to other obligations and lack of prioritizing on behalf of their parent or guardian these young people suffered mentally, physically, emotionally and spiritually. Christian brothers and sisters, it's time to get involved!

It's time to get involved to sharing the Gospel of Jesus Christ, letting our young people know there is someone that loves them unconditionally and that whatever problem they may be experiencing, God still loves them. Oftentimes when we go through painful situations we automatically think God is mad. We end up blaming Him for the problem or we become hard-hearted and turn our backs on Him.

Testimony 4. *Saints, God is always setting up divine appointments. On this particular day the Lord led me to witness to a young man by the name of Bobby. I was not out with a witnessing team, I was with my friend Carla on my way to check on a church member named Lisa. Carla and I arrived at the apartment and pulled up to Lisa's building. We walked up to the door, rang the doorbell and Lisa buzzed for us to enter. After entering the apartment the three of us began chatting about some issues that Lisa had been dealing with. However around 20 minutes after our conversation with her, the apartment buzzer rings and Lisa answers it. Her boyfriend comes into the room appearing to be filled with hostility and making it known through his demeanor. He heads to leave out the front door but before he gets out the door I politely asked him if I could speak with him for a minute and he accepted. The two of us stepped out into the hallway for privacy but still in plain view of the others. (The Bible says that we should always be wise.) The young man and I began talking. Remember that private moment Jesus spoke about with the Samaritan woman? This is a private moment.*

The two of us are now in the hallway and I started out by introducing myself and asked him if everything was OK. Oh how he was waiting to vent some of his anger, and that he did! As I stood there and listened to this young man release years of anger and frustration, I began praying in my mind asking God to lead me, guide me and give me wisdom. While still listening attentively and encouraging him throughout our conversation, it was not long before I had the opportunity to ask him about his relationship with God. He later confessed he was angry with God. Bobby stated that growing up his grandmother took care of him after his mother put him out of the home at age 14. Bobby shared his painful testimony of living on the streets for many years. He often referred back to his grandmother who apparently was the only one who had made an impact on his life, even after her death.

As I continued to listen I must confess my hope for him began to take wings. I stood there becoming angry because at one point he began to insult God and I took that personal. "Bobby," I said, "wait a minute. Let me speak please." Standing my ground for Jesus I began giving an illustration of how Jesus suffered and that sometimes our suffering is caused by choices that we make. However, God still loves us! After I got those words in Bobby took over the conversation once again and I stood there and continued listening.

After about 45 minutes of being in the hallway, I began to feel discouraged as well as feeling that no progress had been made. I asked God if there was any hope for Bobby as I walked back into the apartment. When we walked through the door, Lisa asked if everything was OK? I responded that everything was fine. Carla told Bobby just three simple words: God loves you! (Carla had known Bobby from years ago.) Soon after Carla said those words, the two of them began to talk and Lisa and I left to give them privacy. I periodically peeked in on them to see how things were progressing and after about an hour of ministering to Bobby, Carla and I left, both feeling drained and overwhelmed and thinking WOW! That was truly an experience.

After we left and was driving home, the Holy Spirit said, "All Bobby needed was love. Melecia think about all that he'd been through. Don't ever think that anyone's situation is hopeless! For with me (Holy Spirit speaking) all things are possible!"

Yes ALL things are possible because the very next day – Saturday – I received a message from Bobby on my phone saying that he would like to come to church on Sunday and that he also wanted to surrender his life to Jesus Christ. And he did! The next day – Sunday – Bobby showed up for church looking like a different person. Through the entire service he sat attentively, engaging in the songs and the sermon, waiting patiently for his moment to walk down the aisle of the Church sanctuary and accept Jesus Christ as his Lord and Savior. With God all things are possible.

Bobby received salvation through Jesus Christ and one week later he was baptized! You see one person can make a difference; one person did make a difference, they made an impact because they made the choice to obey. Dear ones if we are willing to surrender ourselves and our time for the mission, God will do the saving! We will experience victory in this win-win situation. As we look back at our last testimony we can thank God for an obedient spirit, as well as a listening spirit. Sometimes all we need to know is that someone cares and they can show that they care just by listening.

Christian brothers and sisters, no situation is hopeless with God. It's time to get involved! Let God use YOU!

<u>Notes</u>

Chapter Six

Faith To

Get It Done

We often hear the question asked what is faith? And then the person will recite or respond with the scripture that's found in Hebrews 11:1; which says, "Now faith is the substance of things hoped for, the evidence of things not seen." Let us now view faith from three perspectives.

The first view. If one has studied the scripture in Hebrews, then maybe that person has a grasped on the meaning of faith, if they have studied it, right? The second view holds the opinion if one hasn't studied about faith, then that person probably only knows how to quote the scripture or quote many scriptures related to faith. They may have also heard others give definitions and or testimonies/life experiences about faith. However, when asked to explain faith they are left feeling they still don't have a full understanding about it. And lastly, our third view on faith is the person who has heard about faith... studied about faith ...and lived a life of faith in God!

Wow, that sounds deep, huh? But in reality what does it really mean? Well my beloved, that statement "lived a life of faith in God" simply means that a person has experienced a life of various faith tests, tests to teach them total dependence upon the Lord! A test that may have positioned them in an unbearable circumstance, or maybe, even an unimaginable circumstance. Humanly speaking, they thought they could have never endured something of that magnitude, the situation seemed impossible to the human eye, it seemed that there was no way out, no way through it, and no way around it, except through a divine intervention from Almighty God! My brothers and my sisters, God can make the impossible, possible!

Daily we are to strive at living a life of faith in God, putting our complete trust in Him and what He has promised us, according to His Word. But, let's keep it real, our faith can be shaken and it will be tested as long as we live. Nevertheless saints, even though it may not always be easy, it is required as a believer. And the inspirational part is that it will be rewarded by God!

I would like to take you back four years to 2011. My husband was a landlord at this time and the economy had just begun declining. Many people within our city began receiving layoff notices, schools were closing down one-by-one due to budget cuts, and our community started a downward spiral. Many people were impacted (including us, a family of five with big hopes and dreams) and were now facing a time of not knowing from where the next meal would come. With little to no income coming in, and scarcity of food, I can recall one afternoon my husband suggested we go to the soup kitchen downtown, he said my friend works there and that the food was pretty good and it's free. I looked at him and smiled thinking of the many times I volunteered my services there to help others, now it was me in need of help! You know God has to break us down sometimes before He can help us rise! Daily we continued to put our faith in God and His Word expecting a miraculous intervention.

I can truly say that it was only by the grace of God that my husband and I continued on with everyday life as we knew it: Church on Sundays, ministry meetings, teaching Sunday school, going to Bible study and faithfully giving our tithes unto the Lord. It was many times my mother-in-law would call my husband to come pick up boxes of food after she had cleaned out her cabinet. Those boxes were filled with food and canned goods to be dropped off at a shelter or to be taken to our charity of choice. She never knew her child and his family were the ones in need. God is a provider!

Weeks later we applied for government assistance, willing to accept any help available. This experience was draining and very emotional for our family and we often felt alone. However, deep inside we knew that we were not. Through this storm in our lives we truly learned to put our faith and trust in God and God alone. During the house foreclosure experience, we often felt overwhelmed and stressed to the max, not knowing where to turn from one day to the next. It was during this time of sadness, depression and uncertainty that grew our faith in God! It was in that time of darkness that God showed us the light of His hands reaching out to us and giving us hope...reassuring us that He was with us...providing our every need...and sustaining us with His love! Yes, that was truly a rough time in our lives but it was a needful time. It was that particular storm that pushed us closer to God. As we leaned and depended on Him as our source for EVERYTHING, He came through every time.

So now I would like to pose this question to you: what storm are you experiencing right now in your life? What wave is pushing you to have faith in the only one that can anchor you and save you from going under? Faith in God's Word is amazing! Our Creator wants his created people to trust Him! We put our faith and trust in the President, our mayor, the weather man, the doctors, etc. etc., but have you put your faith in God? Faith to do, faith to go, faith to say, faith to live, faith to overcome, faith to break free, faith to make happen those things that He said are possible according to his Word! Or have we just settled in fear? Fear of things not turning out the way we expect, fear of what if it doesn't work, and fear of what if God doesn't do it for me?

Every day we put our faith in something or someone. If you have a car (1) you wake up and go outside expecting to see your car and (2) after settling in the driver's seat and putting the key into the ignition, you expect the motor to turn over so that you can be on your way. You just activated faith in your vehicle.

According to scripture faith is belief, trust, confidence and fidelity. Faith is always a gift from God, and never something that can be produced by people. Faith for the believer is "God's divine persuasion" meaning God's point of view and therefore distinct from human belief or confidence (human's point of view). The Lord continuously births faith in the yielded believer so they can know what He prefers, i.e. the persuasion of His will (1 John 5:4).

"Faith is the eye that enables believers to see the unseen." God showed me many dreams of us moving out of our home one year before it even happened. Faith empowers believers to do. Months and months after battling with banks and mortgage companies we were later faced with a decision to keep our home or move and let it go! Through those dreams God prepared us and helped us make a very difficult decision. Our home had sentimental value to my husband because his dad helped him build it and now he is deceased. However, Faith in God and His Word empowered us to trust Him and let go!

Faith elevates believers to go above and beyond the imaginable. With no money to buy a home, yet still holding on to our faith and our trust in God, it was one night the Holy Spirit woke me up to pray at 3:00 a.m. and then later leading me to get on the computer and search for a home. Trusting this unction and God's guidance, I did just that.

Soon I found a few homes that caught my eye. I wrote down the addresses and the next day shared this information with my husband. Agreeing to go view these homes, not knowing where the money would come from, we stepped out on faith to go. I shared with my husband that in all the dreams I had, our next home appeared to be a corner house. Also in my dream, this new home needed a little work. Sure enough the home I viewed at 3:00 in the morning on the internet was a house on the corner, and this house needed a little work. After we contacted our realtor to show us the home, a Christian realtor might I add, she took us to the home and showed us the inside, we immediately fell in love with it, we stood inside the home praying in faith that God would somehow make a way for us to purchase this house. And people, God did just that! Now this is not a testimony of name it and claim it. It is a testimony of God being a provider! And as we continued to trust Him and put our faith in Him and

His Word, it did not return to Him void!

Faith however is always from God and is purely His work – Him working through us! All that we have is a gift from God, with salvation being the Greatest Gift! That is why it is imperative for us to share our testimonies and to share the Gospel message of Jesus Christ! We serve a God that specializes in doing things that are impossible!

Ephesians 2:8, 9: "For by grace you have been saved through faith and that not of yourselves, it is the gift of God not as a result of works, so that no one may boast."

Today you can possess this wonderful gift of salvation through simply admitting you are a sinner, Romans 3:23. Secondly, you need to trust God's Word. Believe that Jesus died on the cross for your sins and rose on the third day with all power John 3:16. Lastly, call upon the name of the Lord Jesus to save you. Romans 10:9-13 says, "If thou shalt confess with thy mouth the Lord Jesus, and shalt believe in thine heart that God hath raised him from the dead, thou shalt be saved. For with the heart man believeth unto righteousness; and with the mouth confession is made unto salvation." For the scripture says, "Whosoever believeth on him shall not be ashamed. For there is no difference between the Jew and the Greek: for the same Lord over all is rich unto all that call upon him. For whosoever shall call upon the name of the Lord shall be saved."

The POWER of faith in Jesus can save ANYONE! The Power of faith in Jesus can Heal, Deliver, Set free, Restore, Revive and Break any chain in your life. God said it, we accept it, we believe it and then we act on it! That is FAITH!

Now go and grow your faith through prayer, reading God's Word and obeying the Holy Scriptures as the Holy Spirit leads. Go and grow through witnessing to others about your Faith in God! Go share this wonderful Gospel news to everyone you meet! It is TIME to put your gift of faith in ACTION!!!!!!!!!!!

Chapter Seven

ROMANS ROAD

COME WALK WITH ME

Romans 3:10, 3:23
"As it is written, there is none righteous, no, not one. For all have sinned, and come short of the glory of God." *Remember, everyone needs salvation, because we have all sinned.*

Romans 5:8
"But God commendeth his love toward us, in that, while we were yet sinners, Christ died for us." *Remember, God demonstrated His love toward us by sending His Beloved Son, Jesus, to die for us, while we were still sinners.*

Romans 6:23
"For the wages of sin is death; but the gift of God is eternal life through Jesus Christ our Lord." *Remember, the price (or consequence) of sin is death. Jesus Christ died for our sins. He paid the price for our sin debt. We receive*

salvation and eternal life through faith in Jesus Christ.

Romans 10:9-10, and 13
"That if thou shalt confess with thy mouth the Lord Jesus, and shalt believe in thine heart that God hath raised him from the dead, thou shalt be saved. For with the heart man believeth unto righteousness; and with the mouth confession is made unto salvation. For the scripture saith, whosoever believeth on him shall not be ashamed. For whosoever shall call upon the name of the Lord shall be saved." *Remember, through faith, accept what the scripture says about sin and that we are sinners, believe that Jesus died for your sins on the cross, and rose with all power and confess Him as your Lord! Speak God's Word.*

Romans 5:1
"Therefore being justified by faith, we have peace with God through our Lord Jesus Christ:" *Remember, salvation through Jesus Christ brings us into a relationship of peace with God.*

Romans 8:1
"There is therefore now no condemnation to them which are in Christ Jesus, who walk not after the flesh, but after the Spirit." *Remember, those who receive salvation through Jesus Christ will not be condemned. On judgment day you will stand before God not guilty!*

Romans 8:38-39

"For I am persuaded, that neither death, nor life, nor angels, nor principalities, nor powers, nor things present, nor things to come, Nor height, nor depth, nor any other creature, shall be able to separate us from the love of God, which is in Christ Jesus our Lord." *Remember, Gods loves you. And that's why...Ain't Nobody Mad Except The Devil!*

Chapter Eight
What is the Difference Between Sin and Sins?

The Bible says in Romans 3:23, "For all have sinned, and come short of the glory of God."

Romans 5:12 says, "Wherefore, as by one man sin entered into the world, and death by sin; and so death passed upon all men, for that all have sinned:"

Romans 6:23 says, "For the wages of sin is death; but the gift of God is eternal life through Jesus Christ our Lord."

Romans 5:8 says, "But God commendeth his love toward us, in that, while we were yet sinners, Christ died for us."

Our SIN (the sin nature that we inherited from the first Adam) for which we have been atoned. God sent his Son Jesus as an atoning sacrifice for our SIN on the cross Hebrew 9:24-26.

Our SINS (for those who are born again) 1 John 2:1 says Jesus is our Advocator for the SINS we have committed since we became a Christian. Through Jesus Christ our sins can be forgiven because of His finished work on the cross.

Sins are specific acts that we commit due to the sin nature inside of us. These sins show outwardly through our Words, feelings, thoughts and deeds.

Sin is the tendency or inclination to sin, or to do wrong that we inherited (was passed down) from the first Adam after disobedience in the Garden of Eden. "This is like an internal sickness." Jesus came to remove the tendency to sin of the human heart. That is to impart a "New Nature." When we are born again, we receive a New Nature through the Holy Spirit, however remember our old nature is still very much alive.

Jesus died on the cross to remove from us the tendency to sin, and by accepting Him as our personal Lord and Savior we get a New Nature, i.e., the Holy Spirit. The Holy Spirit gives us new desires, but we have a choice to follow our old nature or our new nature.

When the Holy Spirit first moves on the inside of us we are known as babes in Christ and we have the responsibility to feed our spirit the Word of God that we may grow. If we neglect to feed our spirit man, we automatically feed our old nature/old man (our flesh) giving more strength to the sin on the inside of us, this sin nature on the inside of us is constantly at war with the Holy Spirit.

People of God let us keep up the good fight against sin through choosing to follow the Word of God and the ways of God, totally depending on the empowerment of the Holy Spirit to help us prevail over sin. And dear one, even when we fall down, or sin, or miss the mark, or disobey or make an Uh Oh, God will forgive us, if we confess that sin unto Him, ask Him to forgive us and know that His grace is sufficient. In the name of Jesus we can get back up again after our mistake and continue on in this spiritual race. There is no sin too big or too small that God's love will not cover. God loves you! Let us hold fast onto our profession of faith in Jesus, knowing that the battle has already been won at Calvary…that through Jesus Christ we are more than conquerors…that victory has been made possible through Jesus. And that's why…*Ain't Nobody Mad Except The Devil!*

Chapter Nine

It's Time to Witness, Let's Practice

Below are different approaches you can take to start off witnessing. Please keep reading...

Soul winner:

Hello my name is _____. How are you today? I'm from (your Church name) and I'm out sharing the Gospel of Jesus Christ. Have you received Jesus Christ as your Lord and Savior?

Soul winner:

Hi, how are you today? Do you know who Jesus is? (Let them answer). Have you received Him as your Lord and Savior? May I show you in the Bible what it says about salvation? (You can use Romans 10:9.)

Soul winner:

Good afternoon, how are you today? I noticed you have a cross around your neck. Isn't the story of the cross powerful and transforming? You know God has done many wonderful things in my life. What about you? Would you like to share?

Soul winner:

Hi. I was wondering have you received your free gift. (They ask what gift?) Your gift of salvation that was purchased by Jesus? Do you know that Jesus died on the cross for you?

Soul winner:

Greetings. My name is_____.
How are you today? I would like to take a few minutes to share some important information with you today please. May I approach you?

Soul winner:

Hi. Do I know you from somewhere? You look familiar. What church do you attend? Are you a Christian? Depending upon the answer you can ask the person if they would like to know how to become a Christian.

Soul winner:

Hello. I'm a Christian. Are you a Christian? Would you like to know more about the benefits of salvation? This can be used with a non-believer or a believer.

Soul winner:

Hello. My name is _____
and I am out today sharing the Love of Jesus Christ! Jesus died for our sins on the cross because He loves you so much! May I show you in the scripture what God says about His Love? (You can show them John 3:16.)

Soul winner:

Hello! Romans 10:9-10 gives us instructions on how to receive a personal relationship with Jesus, have you seen that scripture? May I show you?

Soul winner:

Good Morning! My name is _____.
I would like to leave some information with you today about salvation. Do you know who Jesus is?

You can see there are various approaches that one may use. However the most important advice is to always be led by the Holy Spirit.

As we have the opportunity to share and explain God's plan of salvation, take your time and make sure the person you're speaking to understands you, as this is a very crucial time. Why? Because remember, you are the soul winner and this person's soul is at stake. Do your best and God will do the rest.

God bless and Godspeed

Ain't Nobody Mad Except The Devil

www.ingramcontent.com/pod-product-compliance
Lightning Source LLC
Chambersburg PA
CBHW060657030426
42337CB00017B/2666